LISTENING FOR GOD
THROUGH
JOHN

Lectio Divina Bible Studies

wesleyan
publishing
house

Indianapolis, Indiana

Beacon Hill Press of Kansas City
Kansas City, Missouri

Copyright © 2005 by Wesleyan Publishing House
Published by Wesleyan Publishing House and Beacon Hill Press of Kansas City
Indianapolis, Indiana 46250
Printed in the United States of America

ISBN-13: 978-0-89827-300-7
ISBN-10: 0-89827-300-5

Written by Patricia J. David.

ABOUT THE
LECTIO DIVINA
BIBLE STUDIES

ectio divina, Latin for *divine reading,* is the ancient Christian practice of communicating with God through the reading and study of Scripture. Throughout history, great Christian leaders including John Wesley have used and adapted this ancient method of interpreting Scripture. This Bible study builds on this practice, introducing modern readers of the Bible to the time-honored tradition of "listening for God" through His Word. In this series, the traditional *lectio divina* model has been revised and expanded for use in group Bible study. Each session in this study includes the following elements. (Latin equivalents are noted in italics.)

- Summary   A brief overview of the session
  Epitome

- Silence   A time of quieting oneself prior to
  Silencio   reading the Word

- Preparation   Focusing the mind on the central
  Praeparatio   theme of the text

- Reading   Carefully reading a passage of
  Lectio   Scripture

- Meditation   Exploring the meaning of the Bible
  Meditatio   passage

- Contemplation   Yielding oneself to God's will
  Contemplatio

- Prayer   Expressing praise, thanksgiving,
  Oratio   confession, or agreement to God

- Incarnation   Resolving to act on the message of
  Incarnatio   Scripture

The Lectio Divina Bible Studies invite readers to slow down, read Scripture, meditate upon it, and prayerfully respond to God's Word.

CONTENTS

INTRODUCTION

After the fall of Adam and Eve, God became distant, unapproachable, far off from the human race. But the advent of Jesus the Christ brought God up close to real people. He spoke to them, touched them, challenged their assumptions, and became involved in the messiest parts of their lives.

One of those closest to Jesus as He walked this earth was His apostle John, the author of the Gospel we'll be examining. John was the son of Salome, who may have been the sister of Mary, Jesus' mother. John was also a member of Jesus' inner circle. So when John records and interprets the events of Jesus' life and ministry, we can be assured that he was reporting what he knew to be true.

You'll recall that John also wrote three letters (epistles) to the early church and, toward the close of his life, was witness and recorder of the events we read about in the book of Revelation. According to John's account, the glorified Jesus gave him a glimpse at the events that would end human history.

The Gospel of John, written decades after Matthew, Mark, and Luke, presents to us the simplicity, significance, and mystery of Jesus' words. Each vignette from Jesus' life was chosen carefully to convince us of Jesus' deity and provide assurance of abundant life here and now (John 20:31).

This book concisely packages the good news into the oft-quoted verse: "For God so loved the world that he gave his one and only Son, that whoever believes in him shall not perish but have eternal life" (John 3:16). John's vivid imagery and powerful quotes from Jesus show how His bold commands can make a practical difference in both our lives today and our eternal destiny.

THE WORD INCARNATE

Listening for God through John 1:1–18

SUMMARY

It had been 400 years since God had spoken to His people the Israelites through His prophets. Had He forgotten about them? Had His plan of redemption that He had crafted from the foundation of the world simply ceased?

He had promised a Messiah, a Redeemer, someone to free His people from oppression and to crush the head of Satan once and for all. But there was no hint of redemption on the horizon. The prophets had foretold it, but still God was silent.

And then came Jesus, deity wrapped in human flesh. God Himself entered His creation to show a lost humanity the way back to God, to free mankind from the penalty and power of sin.

God had been preparing His people for this event for millennia. The law and the prophets, the sacrifices and the feasts—all of Israel's history and tradition—had been pointing to His coming so they would recognize it and grasp the fullness of its meaning.

But they missed it.

And many still do.

SILENCE ✝ LISTEN FOR GOD

Relax. Take several deep breaths, and let go of all your busy thoughts. Ask God to open your eyes to see Jesus as He is revealed in His Word.

PREPARATION ✝ FOCUS YOUR THOUGHTS

When do you open your Christmas gifts?

Why is it so hard to wait until Christmas morning?

What kinds of secrets do you have difficulty keeping?

READING ✟ HEAR THE WORD

John's Gospel was written long after the others, possibly as late as A.D. 85 Matthew, Mark, and Luke give us the framework of Jesus' life and works, but John reveals their meaning and purpose. Everything John writes is intended to draw us into a relationship with Christ. For example, John states, "Jesus did many other miraculous signs in the presence of his disciples, which are not recorded in this book. But these are written that you may believe that Jesus is the Christ, the Son of God, and that by believing you may have life in his name" (John 20:30–31).

Because the events surrounding Jesus' birth had already been recorded, John shows us the deeper meaning and reality behind those events in 1:1–18. He shows us that Jesus didn't come into existence on that first Christmas. He was no ordinary baby.

In John you will see some words repeated often for emphasis: *believe* (ninety-eight times), *life* (thirty-six times), *witness/testify* (forty-seven times) and *world* (seventy-eight times). The theme of light versus darkness is also repeated throughout. And all of these are introduced in the first chapter.

Read John 1:1–18 aloud slowly. Pause between sentences, allowing yourself time to soak in the meaning. Then have a different person read the entire passage aloud without pausing. As you listen, ask God to impress a word or phrase on your mind—His word for you today.

MEDITATION ✝ ENGAGE THE WORD

Meditate on John 1:1–5, 14, and 18

How does John 1:1 compare with Genesis 1:1? Why do you think John uses similar words? Why does John use "the Word" to describe Jesus? How else does he describe Jesus? In what ways was Jesus "light"?

John tells us Jesus *was* God and was *with* God at the same time. He also describes Jesus as "God the One and Only" in 1:18. How do you understand the concept of the Trinity? Why do many people feel they have to understand this concept in order to believe it?

> When I was young, I said to God, "God, tell me the mystery of the universe." But God answered, "That knowledge is for me alone." So I said, "God, tell me the mystery of the peanut." Then God said, "Well, George, that's more nearly your size."
>
> —George Washington Carver

Read the sidebar quote by George Washington Carver on page 12. Do you think it's even possible for finite human beings to fully comprehend the nature of God? If we could grasp His nature, what would that say about God?

In what ways did Jesus make God known (1:18)? What characteristics of God did Jesus reveal that weren't evident in the Old Testament?

What did Jesus have to give up in order to be born into this world? In what ways was He limited? How does it make you feel to know that God went to such great lengths to reveal Himself to you so you would know who He is and how much He cares for you?

Meditate on John 1:10–13, 16–17

What do you think the first-century Jews were looking for in a Messiah? If Jesus fulfilled all the Old Testament prophecies concerning Jesus, why do you think so many people did not recognize Him?

Do you agree with the quote in the sidebar at right? What keeps people from recognizing God today?

> People see God every day; they just don't recognize Him.
>
> —Pearl Bailey

Do you think people "did not receive him" because they didn't realize who He was or because they *did* realize who He was but *chose* not to put their trust in Him? In other words, was it because of ignorance, willfulness, or both?

What does Jesus offer to those who believe and receive? What does it mean to be a child of God? Why do you think someone might deliberately choose *not* to become a child of God?

Meditate on John 1:6–9, 15

What do you know about John the Baptist? How is he described by the apostle John? How would you describe his attitude? What was the reaction to John's ministry (see John 10:41 and Matt. 14:1–12)? Do you think he ever considered *not* telling others about Jesus?

Jesus came as light into the world, and He calls us to be the "light of the world" (Matt. 5:14). What would the world be like without physical light? What would it be like if Jesus had never come? What would it be like if we didn't reflect the light of Christ in our world?

> Everyone who does evil hates the light, and will not come into the light for fear that his deeds will be exposed.
>
> —John 3:20

Do you think the sidebar, John 3:20, accurately describes people today? Think about when you were still living in darkness. How did you feel about the light before you encountered Jesus? Who was the "John the Baptist" in your life who pointed you to Christ?

CONTEMPLATION † REFLECT AND YIELD

Jesus had to give up all the splendor of heaven to come as a light to the world. What might God be asking you to sacrifice to be a light to your world? How willing are you to share the news of Christ with your friends and family?

PRAYER ✝ RESPOND TO GOD

Spend some time in silent prayer, asking God to speak to
your heart. Jesus came as light and life. He came to make
God known. How can you make Jesus known? What's keeping you from reflecting His light?

INCARNATION ✝ LIVE THE WORD

John's purpose in writing his Gospel was to move people
toward belief in Christ as the Son of God. Make a list of four
people who are part of your world. What can you say or do
this week to show them Jesus?

YOU MUST
BE BORN AGAIN

Listening for God through John 3:1–18

SUMMARY

The Jewish people had always considered themselves special in the eyes of God—and rightly so. God had chosen them. He had redeemed them from slavery in Egypt with a miraculous display of His power. He had given them the Ten Commandments and the Law. But He never meant for them to be the sole recipients of His grace. His promise to Abraham had been, "All peoples on earth will be blessed through you" (Gen. 12:3).

At various times throughout her history, Israel welcomed converts into her fold. These proselytes were said to have been "reborn" at the time they converted to the true faith of Judaism. The concept of being "born again" was not a new one. But when Jesus told a Jewish religious leader that he, too, had to be born again, it was revolutionary. And he had a hard time grasping it.

God's vast love for people isn't limited to the religious or moral. Jesus came to be a Savior for all who would believe— for all who would be born again.

SILENCE ✝ LISTEN FOR GOD

God has something He wants to tell you today: He loves you. He wants to do something in your life. Spend two minutes in silence, listening for God's voice.

PREPARATION ✝ FOCUS YOUR THOUGHTS

When you were a child, what were some of the rules in your home?

How were your family's standards different from those of other families?

What were some of the rules in your church?

How have those rules changed over the years?

Lectio READING ✝ HEAR THE WORD

Word had gotten out about Jesus. He was in Jerusalem to celebrate the Passover (the commemoration of God's deliverance of the Israelites from Egypt). Immediately preceding His encounter with Nicodemus, Jesus cleared the money changers and merchants from the temple courts. He overturned their tables, and drove them out with a homemade whip—quite a display of zeal for God's house.

When the Jews questioned His authority for His actions, Jesus answered, "Destroy this temple, and I will raise it again in three days" (John 2:19). That certainly raised some eyebrows. And so did His miracles. Many people saw and believed (John 2:23). It was time for an expert to check Him out.

The Jewish ruling council, called the Sanhedrin, was a group of seventy-one experts in the law. They met in a chamber within the temple courts and governed the religious, political, and judicial life of the Jewish people. Of all the social groups serving on this council, the Pharisees were the most scrupulous

in keeping the Law. They were considered by all to be right-
eous and devout, having developed an elaborate system of 630
commands to ensure they never broke one of God's commandments. Nicodemus was a Pharisee, and he went to Jesus to find
out for himself who this man was.

Read John 3:1–18 in dramatic fashion. Choose one person to
read the words of Jesus, and another to read the words of
Nicodemus, and a third to read the narration. Have your narra-
tor also read 3:16–18.

MEDITATION ✝ ENGAGE THE WORD

Meditate on John 3:1–8

Why do you think Nicodemus approached Jesus at night?
What was his original assessment of Jesus? Why do you think
Jesus responded to him so abruptly?

How did Jesus' understanding of the kingdom of God differ
from the traditional understanding of the Jews? (See Luke
17:20–21.) What did Jesus say were the requirements for
entering this kingdom? How would those requirements have
been different from what the Pharisees thought them to be?

The term *born again* can also be translated *born from above*. How does that translation affect your understanding of the term (see sidebar)?

> Being born from above is a perennial, perpetual, and eternal beginning, a freshness all the time in thinking and in talking and in living, the continual surprise of the life of God.
>
> —Oswald Chambers

How do you think Nicodemus felt when Jesus told him he wasn't good enough on his own to enter God's kingdom?

What do you think Jesus meant when He said we must be born of "water and the Spirit"? Does Ezekiel 36:24–27 give you any insight? In John 3:8 the word used for *Spirit* is the same word used for *wind*. How is the Spirit's work in the human heart similar to the wind?

Meditate on John 3:9–12

Nicodemus was supposed to be well versed in the Old Testament. He was intelligent. Why do you think he had such a hard time understanding what Jesus was trying to tell him? Have you ever met someone who was very smart but seemed to be spiritually dull?

Read 1 Corinthians 2:14. Did you find this verse to be true in your own life? What concepts did you have a hard time under-standing before you gave your heart to Christ that now seem obvious?

Read the sidebar quote by Anselm. Do you agree? Why or why not?

> I do not seek to understand that I may believe, but I believe in order to understand. For this also I believe—that unless I believe, I should not understand.
>
> —Anselm

Why should Nicodemus have accepted Jesus' testimony about these spiritual matters?

How did Nicodemus eventually respond? (See John 7:50–51 and 19:39.)

Meditate on John 3:13–18

Read Numbers 21:4–9. This is the passage Jesus was referring to in John 3:14–15. How does this event illustrate Christ's redeeming work on the cross and the necessity of belief?

How do most people define *belief*? List several synonyms for *belief*. How does James 2:19 affect your definition? Why is belief necessary in order to gain eternal life? Why do you think true belief is so difficult?

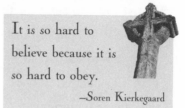

It is so hard to believe because it is so hard to obey.

–Soren Kierkegaard

If we believe in Christ, what kind of life will we receive? Does "eternal" refer only to the length of our lives, or do you think Jesus had something else in mind?

Read the sidebar quote by the seventeenth-century British clergyman Thomas Fuller. How are our lives changed when we truly believe in Christ? How has your life changed since you have become a Christian?

He does not believe that does not live according to his belief.

–Thomas Fuller

Why did God send Christ into the world? How does it make you feel to know that He loved you that much? What would it have meant to Nicodemus to learn that God loved the world? What evidence do you see in our world today that it needs to be saved? What do you think it will take for people today to believe in Jesus?

CONTEMPLATION ✝ REFLECT AND YIELD

Christ came to earth for the sole purpose of giving His life so anyone who believed in Him would be saved. Do you sometimes try to earn your salvation instead of trusting in what Christ has already done? Do you ever encumber others with man-made requirements?

PRAYER ✝ RESPOND TO GOD

Jesus calls us to be born again. Have you been born again? Can you see evidence in your life that God has done something in you? Spend a few minutes in silent prayer, asking God's Spirit to testify with your spirit that you are indeed a child of God.

INCARNATION ✝ LIVE THE WORD

Make a list right now of spiritual concepts you don't understand or of anything else that is keeping you from wholehearted belief in Christ. Ask God each morning this week to increase your faith, to open your mind so you understand, and to make you willing to obey.

SHARING THE GOOD NEWS

Listening for God through John 4:4–24

SUMMARY

E very day at work, at school, in the grocery store, and on the streets, we encounter people who are searching for meaning and contentment in life. If we could see beyond their façades, we would find people struggling with addictions, dysfunctional families, the consequences of poor choices, disillusionment, and discouragement. Some are trying desperately to fill the void in their lives, not realizing that these temporary fixes only add to their problems. What they need is Jesus.

In John 3 Jesus shares the way to eternal life with Nicodemus, a religious and moral man. But in John 4, Jesus offers life to someone completely the opposite of Nicodemus. The Samaritan woman is immoral, an outcast among outcasts. She doesn't come looking for Jesus; He comes looking for her.

In this divine appointment, Jesus provides for each of us a powerful example of how to overcome prejudice and share the good news with those who need to hear it most. And He beckons us to follow His example.

Silence ✝ Listen for God

Imagine that Jesus is sitting next to you beside a lonely road. He leans over to talk to you. What is He saying?

Preparation ✝ Focus Your Thoughts

Think about the television commercials you have seen this past week. Besides a particular product, what were they really trying to sell? What do these commercials reveal about what people are searching for in life?

Lectio Reading ✝ Hear the Word

In 722–721 B.C., the Northern Kingdom of Israel was destroyed by a ferocious Assyrian army. The Assyrians took many Israelites into exile and repopulated the region with exiles from other conquered lands, forcing the groups of people to intermarry. Their descendants were known as Samaritans (from the name of the capital of the Northern Kingdom), half-breeds who were despised by the remaining Jews. Samaritans were considered inferior, unclean, and untouchable. Over the years animosity between the Jews and Samaritans escalated. The Samaritans tried to sabotage the rebuilding efforts of the Jews following the Babylonian captivity, and the Jews destroyed the Samaritan altar erected on Mt. Gerizim in 128 B.C.

Normally a Jew traveling from one end of Israel to the other would make a special effort to avoid the region of Samaria, crossing the Jordan River to the east, and traveling the longer route through Perea. It was rare for a Jew to speak to a Samaritan, and touching an article handled by a Samaritan would make one unclean. But Jesus broke all the religious conventions of His day. He knew there was a Samaritan woman who needed what He had to offer, and He was compelled to travel to a town called Sychar to meet her.

Read John 4:4–24. Have group members take turns reading one verse at a time. Read slowly and deliberately, trying to visualize the encounter as you read or listen.

MEDITATION ✝ ENGAGE THE WORD

Meditate on John 4:4–9

What do these verses reveal about the humanity of Jesus? If you were tired, hungry, and thirsty, how would that affect your willingness to strike up a conversation with someone?

Why do you think Jesus asked the woman for a drink? How did it make the Samaritan woman feel?

Read the sidebar quote by Benjamin Franklin. Have you ever asked a stranger for help? How did your request affect your relationship?

> He that has done you a kindness will be more ready to do you another, than he whom you yourself have obliged.
>
> —Benjamin Franklin

Jesus was in the region of Samaria, which was located between Galilee (to the north) and Judea (to the south), a place devout Jews avoided. He was alone talking to a woman—and a morally loose woman at that. What do you think the religious leaders would have thought of Him if they had witnessed Him talking to the woman?

What kinds of places or situations have you shied away from for fear of what others might think? What types of people are you tempted to avoid? Why? Would Jesus pass them by?

Meditate on John 4:10–15

How did Jesus whet this woman's curiosity? What did He offer her? "Living water" was moving water fed by a spring, as opposed to stagnant water. How is this an apt metaphor for the Holy Spirit (see John 7:37–39)?

Why do you think the woman didn't understand? What was she looking for?

Meditate on John 4:16–18

Why did Jesus tell the Samaritan woman to call her husband and come back when He already knew she didn't have one? What do you think went through her mind when Jesus said that? How do you think she felt when she realized Jesus knew all about her sordid past? Why do you think she continued the conversation?

Have you ever found yourself hoping Jesus wouldn't find out about something you've done?

> There is a God shaped vacuum in the heart of each man which cannot be satisfied by any created thing, but only by God the creator made known through Jesus Christ.
>
> —Blaise Pascal

Read the sidebar quote attributed to fifteenth-century French physicist and philosopher Blaise Pascal. How was this woman trying to fill the "God shaped vacuum" in her life? How do people today try to fill the emptiness in their lives? What is the result? (See the sidebar quote by Marianne Williamson.)

Meditate on John 4:19–24

Why did the woman bring up the dispute between the Samaritans and Jews over where it was acceptable to worship? Think of a time when you tried to share with someone

> Fill your mind with the meaningless stimuli of a world preoccupied with meaningless things, and it will not be easy to feel peace in your heart.
>
> —Marianne Williamson

about Christ. What topics did the person bring up to distract you from the real issue—their need of a Savior? How did you deal with the diversion?

Jesus didn't compromise the truth; He acknowledged that salvation was from the Jews (because He himself came through the Jewish race, and the Jews had the testimony of the entire Old Testament; whereas the Samaritans used only the Pentateuch, the first five books of the Old Testament). But He also pointed to the bigger picture. Worship isn't about a place, but the attitude of the heart. The real question isn't "where?" but "how?"

What do you think it means to worship in "spirit and in truth" (4:24)?

CONTEMPLATION ✝ REFLECT AND YIELD

Have you been harboring prejudice against groups of people because of race, age, economic background, gender, or religion? Are there people you don't want to witness to because they are too sinful? Are you willing to allow God to change your perspective?

PRAYER ✝ RESPOND TO GOD

When was the last time you shared the gospel with someone? Whom might God be asking you to talk to? Where does He want you to go? Ask Him.

INCARNATION ✝ LIVE THE WORD

Reach outside your comfort zone this week. To what "Samaria" can you go to look for an opportunity to engage someone in conversation? Trust God to help you know what to say and how to say it.

THE TRUTH SHALL SET YOU FREE

Listening for God through John 8:31–47

SUMMARY

Several years ago a hit movie titled *The Matrix* was the topic of discussion in many Christian circles. In *The Matrix* most of the human race was enslaved to produce energy for a mechanical world, but they were placated through a simulated reality. What they saw as everyday life was, in fact, an illusion. They were deluded into believing they were free when they were actually slaves.

Many people today live in a similar matrix. They mistakenly think they are free—free to determine what is right and what is wrong, free to do as they please, free to determine what is truth and what isn't, free to create their own destinies. They believe they are the gods of their own universe. Unfortunately, they are deceived. They have no understanding of the reality of life. They're enslaved, and they don't even know it.

Jesus came to reveal the truth. He came to set people free. In John 8:31–47 Jesus gave His listeners a black and white standard that isn't open to negotiation or individual interpretation—not even for us today.

SILENCE ✝ LISTEN FOR GOD

Ask God to free your mind of any thoughts except thoughts of Him. Forget about your to-do list. Let go of your problems. Invite Him to speak to your heart.

PREPARATION ✝ FOCUS YOUR THOUGHTS

Can you remember a time when someone lied to you? How did it make you feel? Why do people lie? Are there times when people would rather hear a lie than hear the truth? When?

READING ✝ HEAR THE WORD

John 7 recounts Jesus' teaching in the temple courts during the Feast of Tabernacles. Jews from around the world made the pilgrimage to Jerusalem for this great feast that commemorated Israel's deliverance from bondage in Egypt some 1400 years earlier. Halfway through the feast, Jesus finally stepped up to teach. And He made quite an impression. The Jews were amazed at His teaching (7:15). Who could have taught Him these things? It is likely that the confrontation in 8:12–59 took place during this Feast of Tabernacles, even though John mentions the conclusion of the feast in 7:37.

While Jesus was teaching, "many put their faith in him" (8:30), so He particularly addresses "the Jews who had believed him" (8:31). As Jesus shares the truth with them, it becomes clear that their belief is not true, trusting faith. It hasn't infiltrated their lives. Jesus helps them see that there is no middle ground when it comes to being a believer. Either you accept the truth, or you believe a lie. You are either a child of God and follow Him, or you are a child of the Devil and reflect his character. There is nothing in between.

Read John 8:31–47. Take turns reading verses, but designate one person to read all the words of Jesus.

MEDITATION ✝ ENGAGE THE WORD

Meditate on John 8:31–36

According to these verses, what is the test for true discipleship? How does obedience to Jesus' teachings help us to know the truth? What is truth?

How do verses 8:36 and 14:6 affect your understanding of what Jesus is trying to say? Once we know the truth, in what ways are we set free?

Compare the two quotes in the sidebar. What is the danger of believing the second as opposed to the first? Why do people today believe truth is relative? How do you see relativity affecting our society? How do you see relativity creeping into the church?

> Truth is eternal, knowledge is changeable. It is disastrous to confuse them.
> —Madeleine L'Engle

> Truth, after all, wears a different face to everybody, and it would be too tedious to wait till all were agreed.
> —James Russell Lowell

Jewish teachers believed that because they had the Law, it was impossible for them to become slaves to sin. According to Romans 3:20, what was the purpose of the Old Testament law?

Why do you think the Jews reacted so strongly to Jesus' offer to be set free? They claimed never to have been slaves of anyone. Were they right? (Think of the feast they were commemorating.) Why do you think people fail to recognize or admit their enslavement?

Have you ever heard people who profess to believe in God make excuses for their lives of sin? List some of the sins to which people today are enslaved.

> Christian, n., One who follows the teachings of Christ insofar as they are not inconsistent with a life of sin.
>
> —Ambrose Bierce

What does the quote by Ambrose Bierce reveal about the way the world perceives most religious people? How does it make you feel to know that people think of Christians in this light? What does Jesus mean when He says, "So, if the Son sets you free, you will be free indeed" (John 8:36)?

What is your reaction to the side-bar quote by Hannah Whitall Smith?

Meditate on John 8:37–42

> I believe it is inconsistent and disagreeable with true faith for people to be Christians, and yet to believe that Christ, the eternal Son of God, to whom all power in heaven and earth is given, will suffer sin and the devil to have dominion over them.
>
> —Hannah Whitall Smith

The Jewish people were descendents of Abraham, but Jesus said that Abraham wasn't really their father. What do you think He meant by that? Is there a difference between being related by birth and being related spiritually? Do you have to be of the

Jewish race to have Abraham as your father? (Read Romans 2:28–29, Romans 9:8, and Galatians 3:29.) What evidence is there that Abraham is a person's father?

Meditate on John 8:43–47

Jesus says if you aren't a child of Abraham, you're a child of the devil. How does Jesus describe the devil? Why does He describe him that way? How did the devil deceive Eve? How does the devil deceive people today? (See sidebar quote by William Shenstone.)

How do the children of the devil become tools in his hand?

> A liar begins with making falsehood appear like truth, and ends with making truth itself appear like falsehood.
>
> —William Shenstone

Look at John 8:38 and 46. How do we know Jesus is sharing the truth, not simply one man's opinion? Why do people refuse to listen to Jesus even today?

In John 8:43 Jesus accuses them of being unable to hear. What does it mean to hear God's Word? According to verse 47, why don't these people hear?

If we truly belong to God, how will people know? Why do you think Jesus uses such clear-cut terms?

CONTEMPLATION ✝ REFLECT AND YIELD

Can other people tell by your actions whose child you are?

Christ came to set us free from sin. Is there some sin you need to surrender to Him today?

Are you struggling to accept the truth of His Word? Settle it right now, and determine to listen and obey.

PRAYER ✝ RESPOND TO GOD

Pray this prayer together, "Search me, O God, and know my heart; test me and know my anxious thoughts. See if there is any offensive way in me, and lead me in the way everlasting" (Ps. 139:23–24). Wait a few minutes in silence for God to answer.

INCARNATION ✝ LIVE THE WORD

To live out the Christian life, you have to hear the Word of God. Make a commitment to spend at least fifteen minutes each day this week reading the Bible. Keep a list of everything God reveals to you, and start obeying.

THE SHEPHERD
AND HIS SHEEP

Listening for God through John 10:1–16, 27–29

SUMMARY

A ruddy youth leisurely strums a harp while reclining beneath a shady oak tree on a verdant hillside. Nearby his sheep graze peacefully. The setting is serene. It's what most of us envision when we think of a shepherd overseeing his sheep. But it's not an accurate reflection of shepherding in Jesus' day.

The hillsides surrounding Jerusalem were rocky, and vegetation was sparse. Water was scarce. Shepherds often faced danger from wild animals and thieves who saw sheep as easy prey. Good shepherds took their jobs seriously and risked their own lives for the protection of their flock.

In the Old Testament, God described himself as a Shepherd for His people (Ps. 23:1, Isa. 40:10–11, and Ezek. 34:11–16). And the kings of Israel, as His representatives, were also supposed to act as shepherds. But instead of protecting the flock, they forsook the Lord, led the people into sin, and subjected them to disaster.

So God promised to send a Good Shepherd for His people — the Messiah. The true sheep would recognize Him immediately.

SILENCE ✝ LISTEN FOR GOD

Imagine yourself alone on a peaceful hillside. Listen. Do you hear Jesus' voice as He beckons you? What does His voice sound like? What does He say to you?

PREPARATION ✝ FOCUS YOUR THOUGHTS

How does it make you feel when someone you haven't seen in a long time remembers your name, or when someone you barely know calls you by name?

Who has a unique voice that you always recognize?

Lectio READING ✝ HEAR THE WORD

Jesus' many-faceted illustration of the shepherd and the sheep was an indictment of the Pharisees and religious leaders who, though supposed to be watching out for the welfare of God's people, showed no compassion and no responsibility in leading them to God's Messiah. This was especially apparent after their treatment of the man born blind (but healed by Jesus) in chapter 9 and their prior determination to excommunicate anyone who acknowledged that Jesus was the Messiah (John 9:22).

The imagery of the shepherd was familiar. During the cold winter months, sheep were often kept inside at night in a walled enclosure. Several flocks occupied one pen, and a watchman was assigned to guard the gate until the shepherds returned. Only the shepherd had rightful access to the sheep. Though sheep were not the brightest animals, they readily recognized their own shepherd's voice and followed when he came calling.

In John 10:11–18 Jesus contrasts the genuine self-sacrificing love of the shepherd with the self-interest and self-preservation of the hired hand.

Jesus also compares himself to the single gate that provided access to the sheep, illustrating the necessity of going through Him in order to be saved. Here the focus turns to the sheep, who must be *His* sheep and must enter *His* way. Jesus clearly defines those who are His.

Read John 10:1–16, 27–29 silently. Then have someone read the passages out loud while everyone else closes their eyes. Try to envision the scenes.

MEDITATION ✝ ENGAGE THE WORD

Meditate on John 10:2–6

What are some of the characteristics of the shepherd mentioned in these verses? How is the role of the shepherd different from the cowboy or cattle-herder you often see in old western movies?

Why would a shepherd bother to name all his sheep? How does it make you feel to realize Jesus knows your name? Can you think of other verses that reveal how God is intimately acquainted with us?

What two traits define the sheep? What does it mean for us to know the Shepherd's voice? How do we learn to recognize it?

Do you agree with the sidebar quote? What are some other ways we hear God's voice today? In what ways does the Shepherd expect us to follow Him? What are the advantages of following the Shepherd? What are the consequences of not following? Read Psalm 23. Why would any sheep *not* follow the Good Shepherd?

> There are four especial ways in which God speaks: by the voice of Scripture, the voice of the inward impressions of the Holy Spirit, the voice of our own higher judgment, and the voice of providential circumstances.
>
> —Hannah Whitall Smith

Does Jesus expect us to run away when we hear a stranger's voice today? What do you think He means by that statement? Who or what does the stranger represent? What does it mean to run away? Describe an experience when you encountered a stranger who sought to lead you away from the Shepherd. How did you respond?

Meditate on John 10:1, 7–10

Who were the thieves and robbers Jesus was referring to? In what way were they refusing to enter by the gate? How did they steal and kill and destroy the flock?

In contrast, how does Jesus treat His sheep (10:9)? What does He offer (10:10)? What does it mean to have life "to the full" (10:10)?

Do you know anyone who is trying to be saved through a means other than by coming through the Gate (Christ)? To whom or to what are they looking for salvation? How can you explain to them the benefits of following the Shepherd and warn them of the dangers of following robbers?

Meditate on John 10:11–16

Here Jesus contrasts the Good Shepherd with the hired hand. What's the difference? Have you seen this principle in life today, perhaps when a business owner and his employees display different priorities? What are the principal concerns of each? If a pastor of a church is a hired hand and not a shepherd, how might that affect his or her priorities and attitudes toward the flock? (See 1 Peter 5:2–3.) As the Good Shepherd, what is Jesus willing to do for His sheep? Why would He do that? How does that make you feel?

Discuss the sidebar quote. Can you think of any examples of something a Christian might gladly do for money but not for Christ? Why do you think money is such a powerful motivator for some people? What should be our motivation for following Christ and caring for one another? Which should be more compelling?

> And I am ashamed to think that any Christian should ever put on a long face and shed tears over doing a thing for Christ, which a worldly man would be only too glad to do for money.
>
> —Hannah Whitall Smith

Meditate on John 10:27–29

From verses 3–4, 14, 16, and 27, define *sheep*. How do we know if someone is truly one of Jesus' sheep? What assurance does Jesus give concerning His sheep in verse 28? The Greek word for *snatch* in verses 28 and 29 is also found in 10:12, where it is translated *attack*. What did Jesus mean when He says no one can snatch them out of His hand (10:28)?

Read the sidebar quote. How does it change the way you understand these verses? Is it possible for sheep to walk away from the Shepherd on their own accord?

> The question is of enemies from without who seek to carry off the sheep, but not of unfaithfulness through which the sheep would themselves cease to be sheep.
>
> —Frederick Louis Godet

CONTEMPLATION ✝ REFLECT AND YIELD

Have you been guilty of listening to the voice of a robber or following a hired hand instead of listening to or following Jesus? Or have you been wandering on your own, refusing to follow the Shepherd or any of His earthly representatives? Are you willing to start listening and following?

PRAYER ✝ RESPOND TO GOD

Do you need a shepherd to guide you, protect you, and save you? Do you want one? Jesus wants to be your Shepherd. If you are His sheep, you must listen to His voice and follow where He leads. Ask God to help you recognize His voice today.

INCARNATION ✝ LIVE THE WORD

Make a commitment to spend five to ten minutes each morning this week simply listening for God's voice. Don't say anything. Just listen. If you are persistent, God will speak to you, and you will learn to recognize His voice.

Assurance of Heaven and the Holy Spirit

Listening for God through John 14:1–6, 15–21, 25–27

Summary

Every day newspapers announce the latest tragedies—wars, bombings, murders, accidents, kidnappings, abuses, and diseases. The casual observer is tempted to believe that an uncaring God has abandoned the world or that He is unable to control the downward spiral of civilization. Our hearts can easily become troubled by the uncertainty of the future and the possibility of pain for ourselves and our families. But troubling times are nothing new. In fact, Jesus confirmed, "In this world you *will* have trouble" (John 16:33, emphasis added). Trouble is a certainty—but being troubled isn't. We can have peace in the midst of turmoil.

The struggles of life serve to intensify our longing for heaven. And heaven is a certainty. Jesus said it was. The Holy Spirit is the guarantee that heaven awaits us. We haven't been left alone as orphans to fend for ourselves. Our God is with us through every trial—through every tragedy—in the person of the Holy Spirit residing within us.

If you don't have that assurance, you can.

SILENCE ✦ LISTEN FOR GOD

The Holy Spirit desires to speak to your heart today as you mediate on His Word. Quietly repeat His name to yourself and wait for His presence before proceeding.

PREPARATION ✦ FOCUS YOUR THOUGHTS

What do you think heaven will be like? What do you envision us doing there?

Make a list of four or five things that you can't see yet believe are real.

READING ✝ HEAR THE WORD

Just days earlier, Jesus had been welcomed into Jerusalem by throngs of worshipers gathered for the upcoming Passover celebration. They had waved palm branches and shouted, "Hosanna!" Excitement had filled the air as word spread that Jesus raised Lazarus from the dead in nearby Bethany. But Jesus knew the adulation wouldn't last. He knew His crucifixion was at hand.

John 13–17 is the most extensive record in the Gospels of the events taking place the night before Jesus' crucifixion. Jesus washed the disciples' feet in a striking display of love and servitude. And then He told them He would die; He would be betrayed by one of the twelve; Peter would disown Him three times before morning. The disciples were understandably troubled. This wasn't what they were expecting. And so Jesus speaks words of comfort and assurance to His disillusioned followers.

Slowly read John 14:1–6, 15–21 and 25–27. Take turns reading, with each person reading one verse at each turn.

MEDITATION ✝ ENGAGE THE WORD

Meditate on John 14:1–6

What does Jesus mean when He speaks of His Father's house? How does His use of the same phrase in 2:16 affect your understanding? The word for *rooms* literally means *dwelling places* (translated *home* in 14:23). What is the significance of the Father's house having many rooms?

Read Ephesians 2:21–22. Do you think Jesus is speaking about heaven or of His coming into our lives in a personal relationship in John 14:1–6? Or is it possible that He has both in view? (See Heb. 8:5; 9:11 and Rev. 11:19; 15:5.)

In John 14:3 Jesus promises to go to prepare a place and then to come back and take them to be with Him. Do you think He is referring to: going to the cross and coming back after the resurrection; going into heaven at the ascension and then coming back at the Second Coming; or something else?

How does focusing on heaven (or on our relationship with Christ) help our hearts to be untroubled? (Read the sidebar quote by Bob Snyder on page 55.)

Read John 14:6. How does knowing that Jesus is the one and only way, and not one way among many, give you certainty in the face of adversity?

Our destination is home with our Father in heaven. It is so easy on this journey to lose sight of our destination and to focus on the detours of this life instead. This life is only the trip to get home.

—Bob Snyder

Meditate on 14:15–21

How does Jesus describe the Holy Spirit? Can you think of any instances in the Old Testament where the Holy Spirit empowered an individual? How was the role of the Holy Spirit described in the Old Testament different from what Jesus describes here?

In Acts 2 God sent the Holy Spirit to fill and empower all the believers at Pentecost. Does He still do that today? How? When? (See Romans 8:9.)

How does Jesus equate himself with the Holy Spirit in these verses? How is His presence a comfort and help in times of trial?

How do we show Jesus that we really love Him (14:15, 21)? What do you think Jesus means when He says of one who loves Him, "I, too, will love him and show myself to him" (14:21)? How does Jesus reveal himself to us on a daily basis?

Read 1 Corinthians 2:9–10. How does the Holy Spirit make heavenly realities known to us?

Read 2 Corinthians 1:22; 5:5; and Ephesians 1:4. What does the Holy Spirit *guarantee* for us? How do we know for sure that the Holy Spirit dwells within us (Rom. 8:16)?

Read the sidebar quote by Gordon MacDonald. How will the Holy Spirit manifest himself if He is truly in us?

> One quickly gains a sense from the Bible that wherever the Holy Spirit is found in the lives of people, strange and wonderful things are likely to happen at any moment.
>
> –Gordon MacDonald

Meditate on John 14:25–27

What is the role of the Holy Spirit? In what ways did the Holy Spirit teach and remind the disciples? In what ways does He still do that today for us? Does this negate our responsibility to read and study the Word or to listen to pastors and teachers? Why or why not?

How would you define "peace"? How is the peace Jesus offers different from what the world offers? According to Philippians 4:6–7, how do we gain peace?

Do you agree with the sidebar quote by A.W. Tozer? Can you put it in your own words? Why would compartmentalizing our lives deprive us of peace? On a scale of one to ten (ten being the highest), how much peace do you have on a daily basis?

> One of the great hindrances to internal peace that the Christian encounters is the common habit of dividing our lives into two areas—the sacred and the secular.
>
> –A.W. Tozer

CONTEMPLATION ✝ REFLECT AND YIELD

In what ways do people become materialistic or worldly in their perspectives of heaven? Are you ever tempted to think of heaven as a place where you can have everything you want? What makes it heaven? How can you experience a taste of true heaven right where you are today?

PRAYER ✝ RESPOND TO GOD

God doesn't want you to be troubled or afraid. Cast your anxieties on Him right now. Then grab a partner and ask him or her, "How can I pray for you today?" Lift your burdens to God together, and ask Him to give you peace.

INCARNATION ✝ LIVE THE WORD

If you lack peace because you are prone to worry, learn to let go and trust God. This week make a list of all the things that trouble your spirit. Pray over a different item each day and ask the Holy Spirit to give you peace.

REMAINING IN THE VINE

Listening for God through John 15:1–7

SUMMARY

J esus came to reveal the Father and to show us the way to a personal relationship with Him. Seven times in John's gospel Jesus says, "I am . . .," and follows with a word picture that reveals both who He is and how we should respond. ("I Am" was the covenant name for God, revealed in Exodus 3:14. But Jesus applies it to himself in John 8:58.) Jesus is the Bread of Life (6:48) we depend on for our sustenance; the Light of the World (8:12) we reflect; the Gate (10:9) we must enter through; the Good Shepherd (10:11) we follow; the Resurrection and the Life (11:25) we place our hope in; the Way, the Truth and the Life (14:6) we believe and obey. And now, in 15:1, He describes himself as the Vine.

Jesus reveals to us the only way to faithfully live out the Christian life. We must remain in Him. We must maintain a consistent, abiding relationship with Christ. It's not beginning well that counts most; it's living and ending well.

SILENCE ✝ LISTEN FOR GOD

Quietly and reflectively repeat the seven "I Am" statements of Jesus one or two times: "I am the Bread of Life," "I am the Light of the World," etc. Which description most resonates with your soul?

PREPARATION ✝ FOCUS YOUR THOUGHTS

Do you still maintain a relationship with any friends from high school or college? Why or why not? What determines whether you keep in touch with someone?

How do your friendships affect your behavior or attitude?

Lectio
READING ✝ HEAR THE WORD

The symbol of the vine was familiar to Jews living in Jesus' day. Vineyards were commonplace, and the proper care and pruning of them was common knowledge. As Jesus and His disciples set out from the Upper Room and made their way to the Mount of Olives, they no doubt passed several. Maybe it was passing the ornate golden vine that adorned the entrance to the Temple that prompted Jesus' illustration.

In the Old Testament the nation of Israel was often likened to a vine—albeit a useless, unproductive one. So, when Jesus announces He is the "true vine," He is certainly claiming to be the true Israel. But unlike faithless Israel, He is not lacking in any way. He is the source of life for all who remain in Him.

In chapter 15 Jesus uses the word *remain* (*abide* in the KJV) eleven times. In John's gospel it is used a total of forty times. Even in John's epistles it occurs twenty-seven times. Do you get the impression the word is important? Remaining in the vine is the secret to a vibrant, productive, fruitful Christian life. It is also the secret to answered prayer.

Jesus never meant for us to have a casual relationship with Him. He meant for us to be constantly abiding in Him.

Have one person slowly read aloud John 15:1–17. Join together in reading the word *remain* whenever it occurs.

MEDITATION ✝ ENGAGE THE WORD

Meditate on John 15:1–8

Who is the gardener? What is His purpose in pruning the vine? When have you felt the pruning hand of God in your life? Was it painful or pleasant? What was the final result?

The Greek word for *prune* also means *clean*. How does that, along with Jesus' words in 13:10, affect your understanding of 15:3?

What does it mean to remain in Christ? How do we do it? What are the indicators that someone is not remaining in Christ? What is the consequence? How does Luke 13:6–9 affect your understanding of this passage?

In John 15:2 and 5, Jesus talks about bearing fruit. What is the fruit of a Christian? Read Galatians 5:22–23 and the sidebar quote by Agnew on the next page.

On a scale of one to ten (one being the lowest), how fruitful do you consider yourself? How satisfied are you with your level of fruitfulness? What can you do to become more fruitful?

> The fruit of the Spirit is the harvest, marking growth and maturity. It produces ethical character. It is the true measure of holiness of life and practice in the believer. Every believer is expected to bear fruit.
>
> —Milton S. Agnew

Do you agree with the sidebar quote by Robert Foster? What does he mean by focusing on the foliage instead of the root system?

Read verses seven and eight. If we are remaining in Christ, for what kinds of things will we pray? What do you usually pray for? In what ways does God receive glory through our fruitfulness?

> The man who concentrates on the root system of his life is going to bear fruit upward, but if he concentrates on the eye-appealing foliage he may end up a rootless failure.
>
> —Robert D. Foster

Meditate on John 15:9–17

How are love and obedience connected?

What are some tangible ways we can show love for other Christians? How did Jesus demonstrate His love for people? Do you think He really expects us to give up our lives for one another? Why or why not? For whom would you unhesitatingly give your life? Consider this question silently: For whom would you have trouble dying?

What is the result of obedience to Christ's commands? What is the difference between joy and happiness?

If you don't feel joy in your heart, how can you obtain it today?

What do you consider the five most important qualities in a friend? What does Jesus say differentiates a friend from a servant?

> The miracle of the joy of God has nothing to do with a man's life or his circumstances or the condition he is in. Jesus does not come to a man and say "Cheer up." He plants within a man the miracle of the joy of God's own nature.
>
> —Oswald Chambers

What "business" of His has Jesus revealed to us? (See John 15:15.) Which two Old Testament figures were considered friends of God (see Exod. 33:11 and Isa. 41:8)? Why do you think they were described that way? What does it mean to be Jesus' friend?

What do you think it means to pray in Jesus' name (John 15:16)? Notice the word *then* in the middle of verse 16. What condition does Jesus give for answered prayer? What should Christians be praying for? What could you do to make your prayers more powerful and effective? (See James 5:15–16.)

CONTEMPLATION ✝ REFLECT AND YIELD

Remaining isn't passive. Are you actively cultivating your relationship with Christ? How can you draw closer to Him? Are you afraid of the pruning process or what He might ask of you? Trust Him. He has your best interests at heart. Let go of anything hindering your walk with Christ.

PRAYER ✝ RESPOND TO GOD

God appointed us to bear fruit. He expects it of us. Ask God today to prune you to make you more fruitful. Then pray for the person on your right.

INCARNATION ✝ LIVE THE WORD

List four or five specific actions you can take this week to remain in Christ.

Plan to do one act this week that will show another Christian your love for him or her.

JESUS PRAYS FOR US

Listening for God through John 17:1–5, 14–19, 20–23

SUMMARY

It's no secret that there is great division in the body of Christ. Denominations abound, disagreeing over doctrines and practical expressions of the Christian faith. Even within individual churches, members are often at odds with one another. All the fussing over inconsequential matters distracts us from the mission of the Church in the world.

This is not what Jesus had in mind. He prayed that all believers would be one, just as He and the Father are one. But the oneness wouldn't be achieved by diluting the message or by lowering standards to make everyone comfortable. The oneness would be achieved as every Christian became one with Christ, sanctified by the truth of God's Word. We see so little unity in the Church today because we see so little of Christ.

If we can accomplish what Jesus prayed for, the world will stand up and take notice; people will realize Jesus really was divine and that He really can change lives.

May it begin in us today.

SILENCE ✝ LISTEN FOR GOD

Close your eyes. Picture in your mind what Christ is doing right now in heaven—praying for you. What is He asking the Father to do for you today?

PREPARATION ✝ FOCUS YOUR THOUGHTS

What team sports do you now play or have you played in the past? What was/is your favorite game's objective? How does a team work together to accomplish it? What is the secret to being good at that sport?

Lectio
READING ✝ HEAR THE WORD

John 17 is popularly known as Jesus' "High Priestly Prayer," a prayer of intercession for himself, His disciples, and all believers. Jesus mentioned several times during His ministry that His time had not yet come (John 2:4; 7:6, 8, 30; 8:20). But now "the time has come" (17:1). It's time for Him to go to the cross, to suffer and die for the sins of the whole world. His arrest and crucifixion are imminent. His followers need this prayer to sustain them through what lies ahead.

Many instances are recorded in the Gospels where Jesus prayed. In what we know as "The Lord's Prayer," He gave His disciples a pattern so they could learn to pray. But this prayer in John 17 is also an example for us. It is Jesus' longest recorded prayer. And what He prays in the hours before His arrest tells us a lot concerning what was on His heart. These same passions should be on our hearts.

Place yourself in a position of prayer (head bowed, kneeling, etc.) as you read Jesus' prayer. Read slowly and thoughtfully, with one person reading 17:1–5, another reading verses 14–19, and yet another reading verses 20–23.

MEDITATION ✝ ENGAGE THE WORD

Meditate on John 17:1–5

How many times does Jesus use the word *glory,* or *glorify,* in this passage? What does it mean to "glorify" someone? How did Jesus glorify God? What was the "work" God had given Him to do? Why do you think Jesus said He had already completed God's work when He hadn't yet gone to the cross?

How can you bring glory to God through your life? What work has God called you to do?

How does Jesus define *eternal life* in verse 3? How is this definition different from what you previously thought? What difference does it make if you stress eternal *life* as opposed to *eternal* life?

Meditate on John 17:14–19

In praying for His disciples, Jesus says that the world hated them. What evidence is there for His statement? Why did the world hate them? What does it mean to be "of the world" (17:14)? How can we be "in the world" and relate to the world without being "of the world"?

In what ways is the Church doing well in this area? In what ways is it doing poorly?

How is this a struggle for you? Why?

What does it mean to be "sanctified"? The Greek word used here also can be translated "set apart for sacred use" or "made holy." What does that add to your understanding of the term?

How does the truth of God's Word sanctify us? (See Romans 12:1–2.) Why would Jesus need to sanctify himself?

Read the sidebar quote by Andrew Murray. How does it help you to understand your responsibility in sanctification?

> Many of God's children long for a better life, but do not realize the need of giving God time day by day in their inner chamber by the Spirit to renew and sanctify their lives.
>
> —Andrew Murray

When we are sanctified, or set apart, in what ways are we noticeably different from the world around us? Why does that cause the world to hate us?

What people hate you personally right now because of your stand for the truth of God's Word? How does it make you feel to know that Jesus already prayed for your protection (John 17:15)?

> Christ laid down one definite system of truth which the world must believe without qualification, and which we must seek precisely in order to believe it when we find it.
>
> —Tertullian

Read the sidebar quote by Tertullian. If all Christians have the same Bible, why do they sometimes disagree over what "truth" is? Why is it important to know the truth?

Meditate on John 17:20–23

Jesus wants us to be united, and He makes it possible for us to be united. Why, then, do Christians have such a hard time getting along? What does it mean to be "in unity"? Why is it so important that Christians are united?

> Christian unity is not found in uniformity, organization, or a particular church, but rather in Jesus and our commitment to His teachings, and living them out in our lives. . . . It is only as we join together with others who look different than we do but share a common love and commitment to the Truth that is Jesus, that we can know the completeness of the body of Christ.
>
> —Bob Snyder

Read the sidebar quote by Bob Snyder. What is the secret to

unity in the Body of Christ? What difference would it make in your family, in your church, in your neighborhood, and in our world if Christians were united for the cause of Christ?

CONTEMPLATION ✝ REFLECT AND YIELD

How can you promote Christian unity? Which strained relationships does God want you to mend?

Are you sanctified (set apart for God's use) completely? What is He calling you to do or to become? Are you willing to follow, even if it means others may hate you?

PRAYER ✝ RESPOND TO GOD

Jesus wants us to bring God glory through sanctified lives committed to the truth, united with one another. Are you living this kind of life? In which area are you most lacking?

INCARNATION ✝ LIVE THE WORD

God's Word sanctifies us so we are not of the world. Keep a record this week of how much time you are exposed to the world's views (through TV, secular music, radio, etc.) and how much time you are exposed to the truth (through church services, reading the Bible, etc.).